W9-DAM-171

This edition is limited to 1000 numbered copies, of which :

FIVE COPIES marked A B C D and E each contain an original drawing and are not for sale;

ONE HUNDRED COPIES marked 1 to 100 contain a signed original lithograph especially created for this edition;

EIGHT HUNDRED AND NINETY-FIVE numbered copies constitute the balance.

This is copy number

707

No part of this book, including any of the illustrations, may be reproduced without the written permission of New York Graphic Society, to whom all applications so to do should be addressed.

Library of Congress Catalog Card Number 61-15770.

Printed in Switzerland 1961

VARIATIONS

by

VERTÈS

VARIATIONS

Drawings, water colors, etchings and lithographs

by

VERTÈS

Text by

CLAUDE ROGER-MARX

NEW YORK GRAPHIC SOCIETY

GREENWICH, CONNECTICUT

The chief obstacle to artistic achievement is slackness. In painting, sculpture, or drawing nothing of value can be created without that continuous tension, of mind and hand, detectable even in works which seem to have been most calmly and thoroughly executed ; a portrait by Van Eyck, a tuft of grass by Dürer, an outdoor fair by Rubens, or a bullfight by Goya.

Where creation is prompted only by willingness or habit instead of by a certain inner fire, where, in this effort of self-

expression which is the essence of artistic creation, passivity or technical skill alone prevails, the work betrays its lack of urgency and, failing to reflect life, loses all communicative impact. The unevenness of many pictures, which seem to be made up in bits and pieces, is nearly always the result of conflicting components, some showing the artist's effective application, his impetus and vigor, while others seem to have been executed in a routine manner with indifference, weariness, and even boredom.

Such unevenness destroys a quality essential to a true work of art : its unity. *It should be emphasized, however, that contrary to what is generally assumed, this* unity *is achieved less by discipline than by a continuous creative impulse, by a state of tension similar to sexual excitement. Body and mind, these two inseparables, strive for a climax which, unlike that of carnal union, is not followed by a letdown. A sensation of pleasure—experienced here, too, and like the other, sometimes closely linked with suffering—accompanies that ardor of the self which, expanding, seeks to make others share it. With the plastic arts, in which means different from those of music and poetry are employed, response is frequently belated. As with the stars, it may take years, even centuries, before a light is perceived.*

In discovering the "tactile values," Bernard Berenson was the first to point out what does, and always will, justify a painter's works. Through his lines and colors the painter

creates a world which, though immobile and different from the other—and this constitutes its particularity—succeeds in influencing the spectator and provoking in him the desire to possess one form or another.

No doubt one may ask how these remarks relate to Vertès. Precisely because, when considering his drawings as a whole, a multitude of images combine into a single image, and one realizes that a latent tension stamps itself on a body of work devoted not exclusively, but to a large extent, to women and love.

Unlike those of many other artists known as humorists, Vertès's women are not merely insignificant beings, unstable, despotic, provocative, childish, utopian, covetous, mendacious, dissatisfied, generous, heroic, detestable, and capable of the best as well as the worst. They are all that, of course, in turn or simultaneously; but further, they constitute the idée fixe which no man can escape, the deified forms of his desire, creatures who are unique, haunting, irreplaceable, even though turned out in countless copies and differing from one another only in minute peculiarities or by their first names. They deprive any man, young or old, of his sound reasoning power, foresight, earnest dedication to material tasks, routine, wisdom, and duties in order to convert him into a dreamer and submit him to a variety of bondages.

Vertès's style and characteristic form of execution become manifest even in his earliest drawings, etchings, and drypoints done at the time of his emigration from Hungary. Without losing his critical sense, he overcame a certain pessimism attributable to his age and an aggressiveness characteristic of the era; the corrosive power which accompanied his vigor subsided quickly when Vertès, more inclined by nature to love than to humor, finally viewed the whims and defects of his fellow men with greater detachment.

The precocity of this self-taught artist was astonishing long before he found his masters in Paris—Forain and, above all,

Toulouse-Lautrec. Without subterfuges, he depicts anything that catches his eye and arouses his curiosity, sensuality, and sympathy. In no way does he hesitate or postpone. His reaction is

immediate. *With daring innocence he divulges what timidity or the fear of scandal has caused others to pass over in silence. He is erotic not because the forbidden fruit attracts him, but becauses he loves love.*

Different from many of his fellow artists who are inclined to lash out, he consistently avoids posing as a judge. Moreover, he constantly identifies himself with his persons, slipping under their skin, smiling at their weaknesses while thinking of his own, and being a confidant and an accomplice rather than a mere witness.

He devotes himself to his mission body and soul; and here I should emphasize the word "body" to stress his intense physical participation in the gestures, expressions, and events which others prefer to depict from the outside either contemptuously or mockingly. Vertès does not laugh; he hardly ever smiles. He remains serious even in the face of the gravest aberrations; serious in the manner of the true voluptuary who knows that pleasure is something entirely different from entertainment and that the human being, while believing himself to be free, is at the mercy, as are his inferior brothers, of eternal forces and fatalities.

To use the term "serious" in connection with activities generally looked upon as light in character may seem paradoxical, especially as Vertès's seriousness always remains natural.

His intuition outstrips any reasoning. He knows from experience that, in his case, the first impulse is the best. It is on the spur of the moment that he does the best work, that is, under the influence of an emotion so deeply felt that he can dispense with the model without being false to it. Anything conceived with strength retains its strength. It is himself whom Vertès rediscovers when asked to illustrate a novel, a story, or a poem.

Every time the feelings experienced by another coincide with his own temperament—as when he interprets on copper or stone authors like Verlaine, Pierre Louys, Colette, Carco,

Paul Morand, Guillaume Apollinaire, Mac Orlan or ancient writers like Longus or Virgil—every time love, pleasure, or anything so defined is the principal motivation, he seems to relive his own adventures through those invented by others. Hence the sisterly bond which unites his various heroines; they belong as much to Vertès as to Verlaine or Kessel, regardless of their age; that of Chloé, Belle de Jour, Colette, Lou, or of Lea.

The nude *plays a capital part in his work*—capital *because it is from the head that the* idée fixe *is transmitted to*

the flesh. *It is this* idée fixe *in man or woman for which Vertès remains untiringly on the lookout everywhere and at any moment in their lives. Several portfolios comment on the activities during a day* (La Journée de madame) *or a week* (La Semaine secrète de Vénus), *to which she who never ceases to provoke or experience pleasure devotes herself from morning to night, and in diverse social settings.*

Make-up, dresses, accessories, ornaments, expressions natural or assumed, those conventionalities called fashion which, to break monotony, add a semblance of newness to unalterable necessities—what effort, what moral and physical energy, what presence of mind, ingenuity, and exertion women devote to one single goal: to please! This, then, seems to be the universe, at once boundless and limited, to which this voluptuary is dedicated. La Semaine secrète de Vénus *is subtitled* Chronique clandestine de 1919 à 1925. *The epithet "clandestine" summarizes excellently an essential which need not be masked to exercise an attraction.*

There are, or rather were, places where nothing remained hidden and everything was offered at any time of the day or night. Like Toulouse-Lautrec—whose spiritual descendent he is—not only in his eager curiosity but also in the keenness with which his pencil defines types, gestures, accessories, and décors, Vertès was very often inspired by these places. His first portfolio, Dancings, *published in 1924, four years after his arrival in Paris, consisted of large-sized color lithographs; it was followed by a series of twelve plates called* Maisons, *published by Pellet, who also put out* Elles. *They show what obsessions, normal or abnormal, can be found inside places dedicated to satisfying the imagination and the senses. Paradoxically, the pathos of what were known, before their disappearance in France, as* houses of illusion, *stems from their being devoid of any illusion. Too easy are the victories won against no resistance, in which pleasure is only unilateral and everything is sold, nothing given away!*

Degas, one of Vertès's great masters—and later Forain— have rendered admirably the sordidness approaching horror

within places devoted to the sale of love (to paraphrase the title of one of Francis Carco's works). Lautrec himself sought in them everything that his physical misfortune prevented him from finding save for professional obligingness. The mixture of malice and a sort of childlike gratitude makes his outbursts almost touching. To Vertès, as to Constantin Guys, such a house is merely an observation post, like any other. What has entertained him above all and animated him are less the female inmates, whom he endows with a certain guilelessness, than the thoroughly obsessed customer, whom he has depicted much more cruelly, dressed or undressed, than his partner or partners.

Changed conditions have enabled Vertès to detect sources of surprise other than red-light districts or brothels. Since the turn of the century morals have continued to change, and pleasure to demand new piquancy. Four years of world war favored all sorts of compromises with virtue. Points of honor and the concept of faithfulness have changed, and continue to do so. A certain magnanimity induced even pure souls to overcome jealousy. Luxury is not the only cause of that lack of restraint which became evident around Paris and all great capitals. The Bois de Boulogne and the bushes of Fausse-Repose screened the exchanges, moves, and counter-moves such as were tolerated occasionally in Switzerland or Belgium during the period preceding Lent. The ancient witches' revels were revived (had they ever disappeared?). A bourgeois type of prostitution,

fundamentally superior because of its unselfishness and appeal to the imagination, sanctions even those most deeply attached to each other watching their mutual infidelities, even deriving an upsurge of their own love from the pleasure, given to their loved one by a third.

Dreaming plays an essential part in this kind of entertainment. During hot nights, cars, concluding a pact of friendship by blinking their headlights, follow each other in silence. Women, scantily dressed or nude under their cloaks, disappear in the darkness and, on the very grass, as in Watteau's

Embarquement pour Cythère, *indulge in one-time embraces with strangers, heedless of the varied risks which add an epic quality to such follies.*

But do not let us try to rival in words the many unforgettable images which Vertès was the first to capture, and whose suggestive power has outlived the period and habits which inspired them. I can think of no one but Pascin or Luc-Albert Moreau,

so unjustly forgotten, who, without triviality but with a lively and sensual touch, comparable to that of a Deveria or a Gavarni, could have thus translated such passion to stone.

Erotic artists—or those so called—easily fall into obscenity and licentiousness. They are explicit rather than suggestive; the role of mystery in love escapes them. Thus their representations, far from being stimulating, leave us quite earthbound.

In writing or in painting, how much tact and poetic feeling are required to keep the mating scene, its overture and afterplay, its fatality, from appearing monotonous or ridiculous! Rare are the artists specializing in libertinism who succeed in putting us in a receptive state, the principal criterion. Thus the Hindu sculptors, the Japanese master wood engravers, Boucher, Rowlandson, Rodin—the most voluptuous sculptor of all time— Pascin and Vertès are never immodest in their lewdness; they make us perceive the true solemnity of the moment when, charged with an astonishing force greater than themselves, humans aspire to the absolute and feel as if they have escaped their own selves.

Vertès also avoids the tone, always more or less hypocritical, of moralizers like Hogarth. Hardly any irony is apparent in the evocation of particularly lewd situations. He reserves his irony for that great booby of a rooster which the human male nearly always is; he needs only to be decked out like a bird to add to his formality and ridiculousness.

It must be admitted that, especially in our climate, the human male is peculiarly handicapped at these brief encounters and his opposite would have to be totally blind not to be amused by the absurdity which almost inevitably accompanies his acts and gestures. Nobody has fixed a more quizzical eye than Vertès on the oddness of male attitudes, that of the monocled club member solemn even on the most trivial occasions, the young premier in evening dress on his wedding night, the obese office manager who makes short work of his reclining secretary, the charging hairy brute, the voyeur tottering in front of a window-pane, or the old man interminably at grips with a fake ingénue.

On the other hand, the artist has fully preserved his pity and sympathy for the other side. Even when she forgets her age, silliness, leanness or stoutness, he continues to accord her a kind of impunity. This philogynist *adores whatever childlikeness remains, even in the most cunning and most mercenary trollops. He admires their ever-present coquetry, their intangible good grace when they are accepted as instruments of happiness, or when one appeals to their sentiments, glorifies them, or adds a touch of the unique or infinite to what is most impersonal or localized in them. With emotion he catches the moment when, however clever at pretending, they in turn attain a climax and, delighted or frightened, experience the release which they give so freely to others.*

To Vertès, every woman possesses a trace of Chloé. Even

when she betrays the male by turning to a member of her own sex (Dames seules), *he saves his darts for the pseudo male with the stiff collar, the shaved nape of the neck, the severe*

tailoring, and has compassion for her who, even when forsaking her lord and master, remains loyal, by resorting to all kinds of excuses and subterfuges, to masculine attributes and prestige.

Vertès steers clear of perversity—and rightly so—because,

respectful of the great illusion without which there is no more youth, regardless of its appearances and in spite of all the complexes described, he recognizes in the carnal act a healthiness which has been so justly stressed by the defenders of Lady Chatterley's Lover—*a book which, naturally, he felt called upon to illustrate and which has yet to be published. This healthiness becomes evident even in the illustration of the immodest* Je n'aime pas, *in which Pierre Louys, a master writer, indulged in such savory incongruities of style by using, as did Verlaine in* Hombres *or* Parallèlement—*one of the works for which Vertès had a most fundamental liking and which inspired him to large lithographs—slang and crude language with undue emphasis.*

Even in a net of vices, Vertès preserves a small corner for dreaming. This inclination to sentimentality is manifest in the illustration which he engraved for Ombre de mon amour, *by Guillaume Apollinaire; in it he gives Lou arms like a swan's neck and fills her with romantic languor. It is equally manifest when, tired of witches' revels and torment, he yields, as in his small apartment frescoes with the flying doves, to the attraction of ethereal harmony—roses, a powder blue, an intangibility and a softness which contrasts with the feverish graphic style of his lithographs and etchings.*

In his murals as well as in his water colors and gouaches, swiftly done, he submits to the spell and tempo of the dream.

Amazons, horsewomen, acrobats, embracing couples, fiancées, Bohemians, harlequins, gypsies, and Pierrots lead an incorporeal life suspended between heaven and earth. Airy washes suggest a fantastic world of mauves, carmines, yellows and delicate azures. During the last war he covered the walls of a cloister with a giant fresco, which was executed in two sittings; in it are assembled seventeen young women, twelve little girls, fifteen horses, and eight angels—all in their natural size.

He enjoyed doing some isolated lithographs on thin paper of a pale blue or a candy-rose color. Abandoning his customary observation posts, he has often been found seeking an origin in the unusual and in the marvels of the circus (one of his portfolios has this title) or the music hall. The monkeys, horses, and wild beasts made him forget the fragrance of femininity and follow with delight acrobatics other than those commonly performed between two sheets.

But he has still other ways to escape. They were suggested to him by a city dear to all, Venice, which he discovered in 1952. His Venice is less that of the Lido or of the Florian, of sunbathing or serenades, than that of the people's quarters, where the gondolas glide along, loaded with fruit or naked children who might have stepped out of a fresco by Tiepolo —a Venice of his dreams which continues to inspire him long after he has left it, and which he still peoples with his longings and regrets.

To him it is a second chosen land, and even more unreal at that. There, men, women, and children wear Pierrot's white triangular hat and fantastic capes; their steps hardly touch the earth. "A land without an army," writes Vertès, "without passports, taxes, and hate," where love is free, where nobody

ever lies, where spouses are faithful, and where painters are not jealous of fellow painters...

That he is pure at heart has been demonstrated by the very large number of drawings which were inspired, before he transferred them to copper, by a book which is a criterion. Very few illustrators, except Prudhon and Pierre Bonnard, have been able to recapture their innocence and freshness.

The etchings with which Vertès illustrated Daphnis et Chloé, by Longus, a work delightfully rendered in French by Amyot, are of uneven quality. A smaller format would no *doubt have been more suitable for this idyl. The charms of intimacy in which the eighteenth century excelled are preferably confined to a narrow space. The vigor and intensity of small sketches frequently suggest more than large drawings, whose glow is dissipated over too large a surface. Small formats —as in* Six étages *or* La Semaine secrète de Vénus— *have frequently been found to be the most appropriate for Vertès's work. With these reservations—and they apply to many books, including the best ones published during the past thirty years—*Daphnis et Chloé *is one of the works in which the artist has surpassed himself. However conscious of diversity, of the unusual, of change, he continues, as we have said, to be as sentimentally and physically loyal to a certain ideal as anyone could be. Happiness—I did not say pleasure—he derives only from inexperienced beings, defiled virgins and those who have preserved their childlikeness. Enchanted by a certain caress of the eyes, a certain moistness of the lips, a certain glow of the skin, a certain wave of the hair, by slenderness and definite curves, Longus led him into a sort of earthly paradise where, beneath the open sky and among the animals of creation, a couple unaware of original sin abandons itself to a primitive animality, an innocent enjoyment of unshadowed delight.*

Here sensuality regains its lightness and divinity, for to Chloé Daphnis really is a god, much like the teen-ager that Vertès himself remembers being. Two beings in perfect fresh-

ness merge their complementary curves, call one another by their hands and looks and, standing, seated or reclining, dressed or naked (to cite the gentle Amyot), lip to lip, seek to become one. The lonely music of the contours conveys in these youngsters such perfect harmony that we seem actually to hear them moving and sighing. This Chloé of 1953, with her rounded face, shining and looking as though she had been sunbathing at Eden Rock, is linked, in our memory, by the childlike pout of her lips, the night-like shadows of her eyelashes, the arch of her back, the tension of her body, to her experienced sisters whom Vertès encountered in the worst of places, following the worst pursuits. This Daphnis reminds us of Nijinsky of L'Après-midi d'un faune. *He possesses the curves and beauty with which, as a faithful interpreter of Colette, the artist had already endowed* Chéri. *Only here, the seducer, still a beginner, plays with a partner his own age. It is laudable, for example, that in doing Lycenion's famous initiation scene Vertès carefully avoided all those details on which so many illustrators have complaisantly insisted.*

These Greek nudes do not differ from those of today. Something in their make-up widens their eyes, brightens the eyelashes, emphasizes the lips—makes this or that little shepherdess look as if she had just left her hairdresser or manicurist. She has emerged chiefly from the painter's dreams. It is she whom we meet again, as a fashionably adorned townswoman and no less undressed under her gown or mantle of a good make,

in the countless drawings in which an ever-watchful curiosity follows her through Paris, London, or New York, submissive to the whims of fashion and, even amidst a multitude of men, remembering Daphnis, whom she believes she will find again in other beds.

Whether roaming every quarter of the capital (Instants et Visage de Paris), *or evoking* Dimanches *(Sundays), or publishing the fantastic portfolio* In Memoriam, *Vertès discov-*

ers, outdoors as well as inside, a multitude of subjects reflecting life and its attractions. The landscape which up to that time had appeared only occasionally now dispenses with figures. With the same decisiveness applied in fixing the Jeux du demi-jour, the thick crayon now tackles buildings, trees, a square, an avenue, or a river. Everything seems to have been caught by surprise, noted in the twinkling of an eye; two tall

American women passing by the garde républicain *on sentry duty at the Elysée, an amazon taking an* apéritif *at the Porte Dauphine, horses being led to the Vaugirard slaughterhouses, a wedding party marching past Montparnasse cemetery. His hand, never hesitant, at once found the right grouping and color orchestration. An entire problem was solved almost before it had been presented.*

The street is a wonderful observation center for an analyst; there, unaware of being watched and preoccupied by their thoughts, men and women appear even more natural than when between four walls. What may be going on in the mind of that elegant woman whom we watch, from behind, taking a walk before lunch along the Acacias? Is she thinking of her youth, whose shape she has preserved? Of her lover who has left her? Of the days when this very street, now empty, was the rendez-

vous of all Paris? Of the automobile waiting for her at the curb, which she will soon trade in for another? Or of her tiny little dog which is following her?

Dogs play no less a part in Vertès's work than in that of Toulouse-Lautrec and Bonnard. An illustrated autobiography entitled Amandes Vertes *(i.e. Vertès) relates the deeds and gestures of his companion of fourteen years, an indefatigable walker, Billy, the wire-haired fox terrier, or the love affairs of Kiki, the dairy-woman's bitch. Entire pages are strewn with sketches of frolicking and gamboling canines, young or old, shaggy or smooth, fat or slim, male or female, with or without pedigree—Pomeranian dogs, lap dogs, Danes, Afghans, poodles, Briards, bassets, Scotch terriers, Russian wolfhounds, boxers, as inseparable from the young mannequin or circus rider as from the daughter of the house or the destitute marquis. They stride through the Bois de Boulogne, Central Park, over the boardwalk of Deauville or any waste grounds. They are seen cuddling in the hollow of a dress or a lap, leaving automobiles, appearing from the inside of muffs (how grateful we ought to be to Vertès for assuring the survival of outmoded fashions and words, just as we are to Lautrec for preserving for the present the lace-trimmed trousers, the high corsets which were so reluctant to disappear, the button boots, boas, scarfs, and so many more cherished items of the past!). They pursue their own kind and participate in collective orgies.*

In many lithographs the dogs provide an excuse for the most even or uneven of blacks, and in a number of drypoints, the spot where the burr is the most full of ink. Frequently the opacity of their fur contrasts with the whiteness of the naked bodies or, on the contrary, corresponds with that of the hair and the moist areas, where most of the shadows are concentrated.

This predilection for the canine race is easily explained; while, as we have said, Vertès is not, in the pejorative sense of the word, a cynic, *he is feverishly sensitive to everything that moves, everything that happens, everything that exudes a scent of life.*

If dogs could only talk! What wouldn't they tell us about their masters, especially about what they dare to do and say before them, about their complexes, about their obsessions and their boredom! Is it to escape their loneliness, once again to exercise tyranny, to give themselves the illusion of loving and being loved beyond any selfish motive, that these masters, hardly masters of themselves, are so attached to their companions in misery?

If chairs could only talk! With Vertès they do, like all inanimate objects. Destined for humans, they evoke a human presence even when empty. In the alleys, in the squares, and amidst the shrubbery of the Bois de Boulogne they gather in twos or in groups, commenting on all they have witnessed in the course of a day. (I dream of a series which Vertès would call La Journée d'une chaise, *which would bring to life the mornings peopled by nurses and children, the hour when* midinettes *open their lunch bags or when the bricklayers meet, when old maids seek consolation in a book or when statues fall into shadow, and, finally, the nights when sighs rise from every alley.) Sometimes the chairs lie upturned or reel like drunkards; sometimes two are chained together. Vertès has great affection for these rustic seats, so "elegantly calligraphic" that their very old-fashionedness adds charm. He also likes their counterparts, the benches, which make the alley hospitable, the alley whose curves suggest those of a shoulder or a hip and (as Vertès puts it in a summary of his preferences)* "everything that is round in a woman."

Any work done with such fire is inevitably uneven. In an

output of such abundance, subject to the demands of publishers, current events, and fashion, it is easy to distinguish between creative outburst and what admits to the pressures of the moment. Yet the artist must be credited with the unusual merit of never having agreed to illustrate any work which did not reflect his own feelings. Co-operating with poets—and this term applies to Colette, Mac Orlan, Morand, and Kessel as well as to Verlaine, Pierre Louÿs, Apollinaire, or Francis Carco— at a time when so many modern painters hesitate to submit to the confinement of a text, Vertès excels at drawing inspiration from the action described or from a surprise gesture of the author's—like an action he himself had experienced or a gesture he had witnessed. It is with regret that he sometimes makes a concession to the taste of bibliophiles and heightens, discreetly at that, by two or three additional tones a plate which would have been even more intense in black and white. As Baudelaire said of Daumier, when one has a drawing that is naturally lightly colored, additions of blue, mauve, green, or orange seem ornamental and superfluous.

Vertès touches us most when—engraving on copper or stone—the intensity of his nervous energy, transmitted to his needle or thick crayon, enables him to graduate his strokes from the deepest black to the finest, most ashen gray. Thus many plates of Maisons, La Journée de madame, Les Bucoliques, Promenade dans Paris, Scènes de la vie moderne,

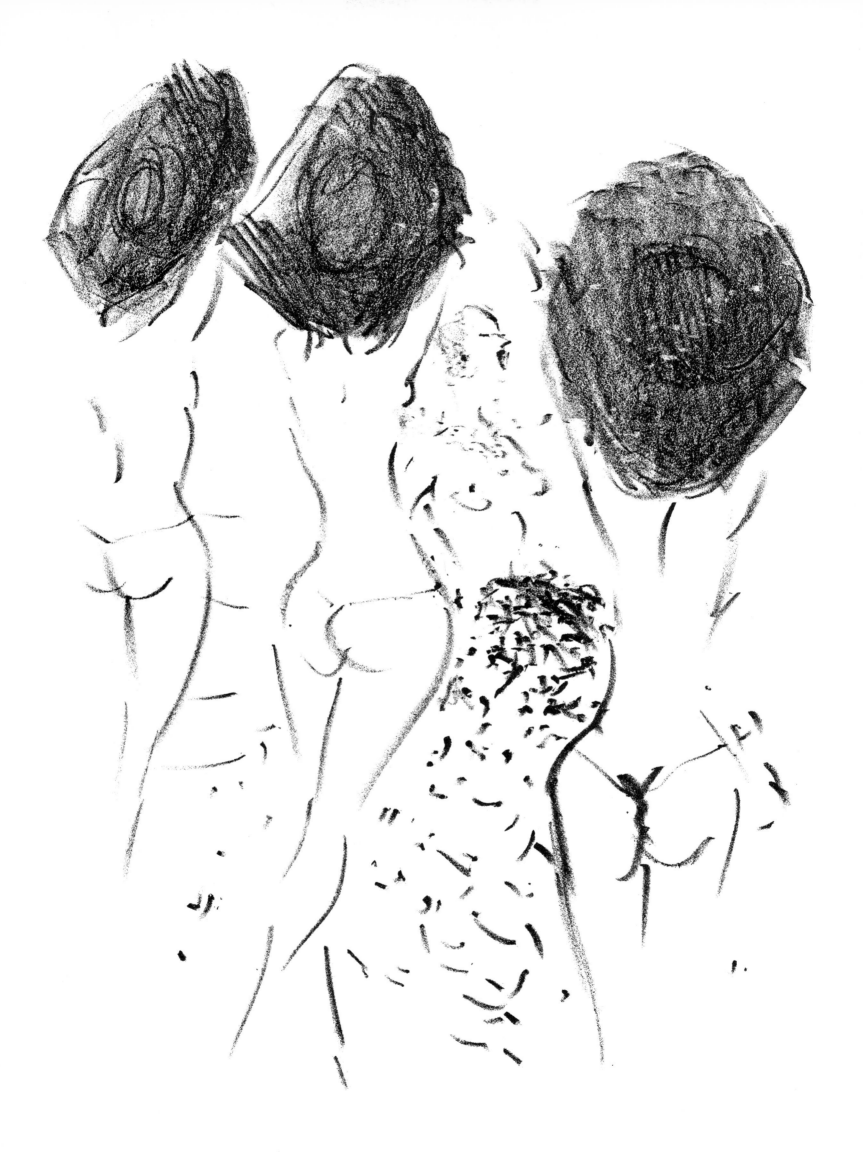

show subtleties reminiscent of Lautrec and Whistler. Take the delightful young woman with the feather headdress, younger sister to Marcelle Lender or Brandès, whom Gérard Bauer evokes in these terms: "What may be her thoughts under the swaying headdress, her eyes lowered to her nose, where its nostrils quiver slightly when she exhales her cigarette smoke?"

Elsewhere large transparent flat areas, done in pencil, shade the original contour. The subtlety of execution further sharpens the uniqueness of the gesture or scene. Forgetting unessential details, the memory has retained only the characteristic aspect which defines the action and gives the surroundings their proper color. Note in Promenades dans Paris *Gérard Bauer's* delicately brushed portrait accompanying a particularly evocative lithograph:

"What happy achievement and liveliness there is in the image of this young girl making a telephone call from the washroom! She is truly at home between the pay telephone and the barely closed door of the w.c. This sketched anecdote reflects the values of life, defining one moment from among a

47

thousand others. We shall never again forget this hotel child who confides her tricks and secrets to a telephone."

Frequently inspired by previous experiments, the etchings still reveal an impulsiveness of design strengthened by the vigor and frankness of the bite. And here again the masculinity of the drawing suggests a comparison with sexual penetration.

Even where the engraver shows momentary lack of constraint, haste or, rather, a good-natured charm such as contributes notably to the unbridled verve of Aventures du roi Pausole, in which the artist—who, incidentally, was charged with creating the costumes and décors for a motion picture based on the same work by Pierre Louÿs—shows that "one pair of buttocks more or less does not matter" (as Renoir said so drolly of Rubens), his spontaneity makes him reject any editing or clever expedient in printing. We appreciate this honesty which enables him to head straight for his goal without letting any retouching or second thoughts detract from his ardor.

I can think of only a few modern painters who would have been similarly able, with a sureness reminiscent of Japanese wood engravers like Utamaro or Hokusai, to conjure up nudes in a single stroke.

Should I mention one of the most daring plates, showing an adorable young girl, nude on her bed—one of her hands conveying precisely the pleasure which the reading of a letter is giving her? Or the many pages of Daphnis (for example, the

cover on which the harmony of two kneeling bodies blends so deliciously with the virgin paper)? Or, for that matter, the many delightful drawings in which the ink seems to lose all weight and blackness, so well does it evoke the translucence of the flesh? What seductiveness is in these child-women, half nymph and

half Parisian, who gambol and seem to float over the ground on airy wings which stress their curves, or dance, spreading their fragrance about them! Here, they are led joyously by a tiny faun; there, they hold a dog on a leash, or are followed by a grotesque figure or a goat as naked as they. Then again, they are seated and breast-feeding near an endearing dog or a friendly foal; here, playing the guitar; there, holding a rose between their teeth; elsewhere, feeling the fullness of their breasts or the line of their bellies; or, under an elm, conversing with a satyr accompanied by a ewe, a bird, or a squirrel. Even in the arms of Lot these girls, made for joy, maintain an air of innocence and divert the artist from the gloominess and restlessness which he might find within were he no longer haunted by them.

Let us praise Vertès for being so little undeceived in spite of his experiences and notwithstanding the folly which he continually discovers in all the great world capitals. One of these international aberrations has inspired him to a recent portfolio: Chez les abstraits. Here, as in Dames seules, Complexes, Existentialistes (or beatniks), he proves his quickness at repartee and a conciseness with words which equals that of his drawings. Remember the caption in Dames seules, "I love you because you remind me of my father"; or in Complexes, "I don't know how to explain it, Doctor, but I have a strange fear of lions." In Chez les abstraits, in the center of the studio, talking with *a distracted model or surrounded by his admirers, the painter has been cornered, compassionately, for Vertès is well aware that among the victims of abstract art are some mystics and martyrs.*

Here, the little naked model, baffled by these graffiti or sketches, exclaims: "Why do you need me for that?" There, a physically impressive playmate innocently explains to the chorus of snobs: "Who would believe that he has never touched a brush before?" The worried dealer: "I wonder whether his vertical period will be as great a success as the horizontal one?"

Abstraction, that epidemic disease, promoted by the Knoks of art, today rages through entire areas of Paris, New York, London, Zurich and Amsterdam. It has infected not only the art dealers, the art lovers, and museum curators, but also the embassies, Unesco, and even the clergy.

There is no more effective antidote to certain viruses than humor. By being right, Hogarth, Rowlandson, Daumier, and Forain finally triumphed over the worst vogues. Vertès, after having denounced so many others, has now dared to challenge the most pernicious of modern conformist dogmas. Like all fashions, abstract art will have long since disappeared, its riddles, its old proofs, long removed from private or public interiors, when his drawings will still provoke a smile.

Thus this great "voyeur" reminds us once more that, regardless of whatever we may be deluded into believing, one of

the highest purposes of art is to bear witness to the life which passes by, *to those singular and perishable forms which a certain epoch of humanity imparts to its sentiments, pleasures, and morals, to the useful as well as to the useless, to its expressions as well as to its language, its dresses, its hats, and to its dreams. And if Vertès's drawings, even though he recorded many actions and gestures which already seem to belong to*

another era, are certain not to become antiquated or, more exactly, to do so gracefully, it is because, behind this modern "new look" and these superficial changes, the philosopher and the poet have never ceased to stress, in man, in woman —united or apart, aroused or tender—in every living thing, and in every sight, what is most universal, most fixed and immutable.

Claude Roger-Marx

January—April 1961

Je suis loin de posséder
un tempérament tranquille,
aussi j'ignore la douceur
du repos. Ceci s'applique
également à mes mains,
elles s'ennuient dès
qu'elles sont inactives,
ma main droite
cherche toujours à atteindre
ce qui est à sa portée
plume, crayon ou pinceau.

*

Je dessine sans effort,
aussi facilement qu'on
sifflote l'air d'une

chanson, ma plume
s'élance sur le papier
lisse, tel un bon pa-
tineur sur la glace,
pour tracer des lignes
droites et des
courbes, sans
que mon esprit
se concentre
sur ce que
cela pourrait
représenter.
*
Les dessins.

Je les regarde comme
si j'étais
un autre
qui obser-
vait par
dessus mon
épaule toutes
les métaphores
qui coulent
au
bout
de
ma

V.

plume.

*

Mais cela ne
peut s'appeler
ce que l'on
entend
par

doodling en Anglais
et que l'on peut
traduire par
"Griffoner au hasard"
Ma main etant

Celle d'un professionnel, reste disciplinée, même dans les moments inconscients. Ce sont en réalité des instantanés de mes pensées immédiates. Je possède un moyen de transmission directe partant du cerveau jusqu'à la pointe de cette plume. Quelque chose comme un asservissement à mon insu, par pure réflexe

~ ~ ~ ~ ~ ~.

Vasto

LIST

OF

ILLUSTRATIONS

VARIATIONS by VERTÈS, designed by Henri Jonquières ; text set in letterpress and illustrations reproduced in offset lithography by Imprimeries Réunies S.A., Lausanne, Switzerland, through the Société Française des Presses Suisses, 9, rue de Clichy, Paris 9e ; French edition published by Jacques Vialetay, Editeur, Paris.